A Tree Beyond
Telling

By the Author

Out Beyond the Bay
Moons and Low Times
At Winter's End
To Hear the River

A Tree Beyond
Telling

Kenneth A. McClane

Acknowledgments

With the exception of the section entitled "The Halves Are Whole," all of these poems were first published in *Out Beyond the Bay* (Ithaca House); *Moons and Low Times* (Ithaca House); *To Hear the River* (West End Press); and *At Winter's End* (Emerson Hall). I would like to thank Baxter Hathaway of Ithaca House, Alfred Prettyman of Emerson Hall, and John Crawford of West End Press for their kind permission to reprint the poems which comprise this volume.

Poems in this collection appeared in *Beloit Poetry Journal, The Black Scholar, The Black Review, The Crisis, The Cincinnati Poetry Review, Callaloo, The Cape Rock, Epoch, First World, Freedomways, The Grapevine, The Greenfield Review, The Ithaca Journal, Northwest Review, Nimrod, Obsidian, Pequod, Rainy Day, Stone Country, Stardancer, Third-Eye, Thoreau Journal Quarterly, Wind,* and *Watu.* "The Judge" was reprinted in the *Anthology of Magazine Verse and Yearbook of American Poetry,* published by Monitor Books.

Copyright © 1983 by Kenneth McClane 4/10/95
LC #83-73442
ISBN #0-933296-10-X [Soft Cover]

Printed in the United States of America

Published by The Black Scholar Press, Box 7106, San Francisco, CA, 94120

for Gwendolyn Brooks

A Tree Beyond Telling

for Gwendolyn Brooks

This is about a deer as he yanks large into the hills.
It is about symbols. It is about everything
which dances in the brain. The dead voices.

This ground lies unbelievably fallow like a poet's dictum.
Always there is but one singing, a thousand
minor crackles, a few
who've suffered the world like a leper.

Such sadness calls presence to hide behind the least
music. It seems forever
The deer will not allow this: he circles back.
He circles
as I shoulder my gun. He surrounds
like a grim lover: all language and retreats.

Until thought awakens
the suggestion which promotes him as a dream
(like the tempering of a ghetto)
must be held, believed.
But like the tree on which our cross hangs
it is beyond telling.

Yet something always saves
the groundless. Look: it is in the hands, the trigger
the lightning pulse
when the dreamer sees again
that Oh
in a world of swimming forms
it is a dark season to take.

Kenneth A. McClane

CONTENTS

OUT BEYOND THE BAY

Presence

Now the wind
turns the rich humus

and shows insides
full of origin

I see:

Indians of the hilly shore
girth with hook, cuttlebone
and whale

and:

a broken cutlass, length of hair—
rope, still combed with sheen and pliant

but now,
someone is coming
his hands are slight and open
as if sowing the clouds

there will be plenty,
plenty for all.

For Saunders Redding and Myself

your words drift at the level of faces
        the language subtle moves like eyes
to the tree outside of window
    and you are talking of Richard Wright
to the trees

            to the ageless bark
                to an oak that by its own green
            profusion cannot be hidden
        and your eyes never drift to the lowest
as some have
    who have been called beggars
                because they could not count on

    trees

            could not count on the undoing
        of what had been done so well
by faces
            and your eyes motion again
        to the highest warp in the ceiling
            to the place of fields
                                not France and Germany
                where Wright gave and was taken

listen to his soul
listen to his soul
listen to his doleful soul

Outsider   (out/side/her)
    but freedom is defined from within
we know that Richard

                        come listen to the wind

                your trees branch overcome with wind
        the leaves apologize for their indifference
                and fall
                    and Native Son was the book all had read
                all on that level in the inside

your eyes lecture better than words
words
I know them well
    fall with wind
but your eyes so stoic
        reach for that tree
                    at the outside
past the corner of 125th Street
past the Ivy of universities
past the faces you don't know
past the face of Richard Wright
past the containment of walls
of the structure
you almost feel free
in.

Dancer

a needlepoint
of mischief
stirring
in the stomach
of a dancer
lends some surprise

a sleek weaving
she quivers
into swift
hoists of toe
and climbs of
arch in her
back so
controlled so
perfect—
an assemblage triumphant
with mechanism, commanding order

I wish
I could
catch her
slipping

for one mill-second
see
the matrix of her
poised leaning
broken
the condition
of her timed-flux
interrupted with
flurry

then I
now content with reality
would let her
brush the moon
again.

MOONS AND LOW TIMES

Driving to Romulus

Out near Ithaca
and Cornell
beyond the great lake
and Taughannock (falls, the
Indians called: "great in the woods")
Out: beyond all this
beauty and out beyond
the seamless world margins
(the universe is bound
     in the shrift of leaf
and the charity of stone & fireweed
     and further in the pointy
          coolings of lovers)

and there is Romulus
US Army base
big in the hills
and bigger than the hills
for there are great

vats and rooms (housing
     for the outcast:

          I am one and will
     always be one
          as I stop
               to look
at other things: albino, skategut
     and fishwife — I'm lost
          in the forgotten) and in

Romulus, unlike Rome, down the road, someone
    may hear the voices of millions
that have not dangered there; have not
    loned in their macrocephaly (better, big-headed)
that the day is done, over, interred:

concentrate: concentrate on the big storage
shed, big, so big, that one may not
pencil its corners or divulge its
absences (so descantive is the warble
of thought—and one may die)

and we shall all take the train
to Romulus
which is, as they will tell you
only a quiet, stony waiting place
with big rooms and gas

and we shall all come (all different and pitiable one)
                and visit
this place and give it voice for a night or so:
    such as we may be allowed

and the Indians called it "great falls in
woods"—called it in a language
that took
a rifle to sniggle it out: to make it only a small cove
a fern of speech

lasting is what the world is about
and Romulus, Rome and Wounded-Knee
    all a mid-form, a stopping (and it is the mind
            that has scared us, escaped us
                and brought us
                hard to growths
                    that coddle like vines)

9

and still laughter (as if we could sin
    and sing)

and still lists: pennywort, eyebright, trout-lily—
    weeds to call the beautiful slight

and the well-wishers are broken, mashed, histrionic:
    blown heavenward so that their minds are
lame, dwarfish, raw

their homes are hovels, small moments—all in
    a syrup that will
        ooze over kingdoms
    and force us
        downward

THE WAY OF THE WORLD IS DOWNWARD

and all   I speak of the little
and all   I speak of the meek
and all   that churns us

        there are some stillnesses, some places of absolute
            quiet
            that need not be filled.

Hedgerow's Dragging Path for Rochelle

The Hedgerow is not and evening's constant
When darkness comes
The low, pursed feeling of raw self
Is a poor survival

And I have gone by the river walking
Walking the long, newsless baneberry shore
Where often we took each other

And thinking of you
like the eye of a boat
I have fallen
As dark water swamps the thirsty
Holes and deep roots

You come
When the wind seems a groaning seed;
Bird an addled rise on the land
And always
I wish the smallest desire came high

Like a city deep in the hedgerow
A crisis
Culls a branchy resurrection, is
Big in a way that nothing can

And always
When sound takes a dull, flat sweeping
Heavy on the river's musk

No One May Rest

When morning is slow
     over the hill and stony birthplace
and day hunkers
     almost lame
in the pines

you should reserve
     your utmost
eloquence
     take the lone sweetberry
before it dries: loosen the suckling
     trail of spanish mossy moon (my naming of
        a crucial feeling, but still
           like moonseed or primrose
             swelled to
             quaint bee & busy he is
                for jam)

out in the wind's
     thawing resonance:
still in warbler nested cedar, next
     in the shadbush
and the gnomes (almost like a city flower)
          of disfigurement—not basswood:

watch the shanked
     spars of bough runnel through the night: celebrate
with all you can muster: noise, body, and wine: it

is a quaff of lading: but even—I may
    at least quarry this—even the wormed places
bereaved with onceness, clotty with age &
    brittle spines—even these have a rueful

sorrow and perspective:
    the economy is half the darkening, dormouse
        world

knowledge is the movement
    outward of meekness, the sea's
webbed edge

the loess (parched, raddled, caterwaul) when the
        poetry
    stammers like tonight
or the morning riotous
    when the baby spurns up his eggs
and his ribs will have
    ghetto no more

I can't say that the boys
will live: life has a sacrament
and sail-furled logic (the puffs

reedful, bogged of their carrying): I
meant to speak of song dust, april
cowbane and the poor that point out the earth

THE FOLLOWING IS ONLY MINE:

WHEN THERE IS
    AN OCEAN
LARGER THAN THE STONE
    IT WAS FOUND UNDER, ONE

BETTER FIND ANOTHER STONE,
    OCEAN, OR HAVE A BIGGER
THOUGHT

and the evil/and the good
and evil/good
and the evil and the good

and god is in the moon, heart and dusk
of our turning: it is a new relevance
    collect yourself—there is
        much to do.

Lust

Anne sits
    with the sun
       and the corn (high and hillish)
    is aging, telltale:

her eyes like silverleaf, loose and weedy, full
    of mornings and getting
coffee, small talk, table pieties

she'll walk out back
    smooth the hens, turn her
ribs on city chores—sweeping and frowning,
    she'll tell you and

then, when you least
    expect it, she'll show

you a thing or two: there's
    a place she'll
take you—go easy, let
    her lead the way

when you just
    get tired and lusty
       she'll stop you

and her voice will
    let the cane
come and go.

Keepsake

Without a clear understanding
    of our undertaking
we should repair back: and in the woods
    of our generality (long horseweed, bushy
coneflower, some prizewinning, perennial poppy)
        everything
      is a presupposition like fruitfly, camps of
        meadowlark
        and sunflower: but still

our argument is our profaning: we have
    eterned by calling this small
and that weak and some (like bluets in camphor)
        mawkish
    and jabbering among
  pines and souls; and others
of some clarity, some hair of class, some
    indication of free-spirit or frenzy
and still
    going as we do
(downward and outward)
    some must be wretched
and horn-rimmed; others must be cast
    to be pitied or made spineless, addictive, shallow
      without equator or rundle
    or water-weary

      but the road by the fatty maples
is quite a gathering
    and all the way with shadows
thrust like oceans or bones kilned
    to dust
and liquored with heresy—

    our deadwords of order (as if tribunals
could stop a slow, warsling fog)
we come
    and darkness shins the last floating
fir:

and the pretty gorged
    under our feet (aye, the sounds)
but no sight anywhere
    as the life noises out of life (mortality
        with such a rough, shabby eulogy):
and what could be grass, mud-snail, or acorn
    could be viper

and now all names
    are of others
and voices bray
    till light
twists in a cold hill
    and grabs us.

AT WINTER'S END

Aunt Lil As She Walks on the Beach

It would be nice if you'd walk
this evening. Nice.
Your aunt looks much better.
I can see how she keeps up; her ankles
run gravelly have summoned
an accappella, a low
wide tongue
that roils beyond belief, is held
where the beach surfaces
past endogamy, sea-oak, blowfish
and lower
where the world works
the marsh is jazzing
(you've loved her always: she's small
and cutthroat) mind it
she's your aunt—no funny stuff!
She'll jitney with that unpardonable swagger
briny like
sex
(oh, love dangerous, oh, how it soaks the rib)

She falls
slowly on your name. Mouthing it
after a long jog
she seems pleased with its silver. Keening
she reminds
of long drives to the charhouse.
How, when you were young—even younger
she seemed like an ever widening presentment:
an acre where roots reach
but the stalk, the timing
of air and corpuscle
is like a lame swimming, a hawk's cry

20

Nothing is wrong: you like her
when she's bottom full
and daisy odor swivels
from her hip
you're happy; happy that someone
is on center

And now as she looks at you
and the sun troubles in her gut
her runny laugh
risks
like a gun toting slave

and now in her winetaught strayings, her back
longing for the horizontal, longing
for that breached hiatus
when the wind stills and he
(lost for the first time) waits:

And you know
as the shores wheel like a moving target
she'll come mid the dunes
and it might be someone old or fat
thin or light-headed
someone who hates the woman she is
someone of a brighter
truce

but probably
she'll rise mid the dunes
with more
than all the sinking

Sunflower

Oh how lovely
is the sunflower

because something
so deeply glimmering

has turned daylight
into an enormous mirror

At November's Turn

Now I am worrying
that the last maple might
thin forever, the grass
burn back beyond its re-investive
stubble, the soul (which somehow

breaks with loss, splinters
with each maintaining) may not
withstand: for always pain
is deadly and not remote: always
like a child who holds
a secret so big, large, weighty
that his parents
rise like a chorus: his sins plain, inexhaustive

And so pain
creeps into the fingers
and claims the gut: and downward
in the last territory, the last salvage
something, cries *no, no, no* not this time

and the world works up barren, stark
dangerous as a friend turned rapist:
and nothing may save you, nothing
can make this thing less sharp, less
infective:

and the maple sits
while a red, splotchy bird
rubs into its branches, and nothing
is seen, seen, though the heart
might wish it so.

Ali

It is that day, finally, when you
    hungering for it always (probably happy, oracular)
can walk out: knowing
    it has finally come, that the asterisk
of dynasty is never
     as summative as we imagine—that the world

is never as nordic, naked and unyielding:
       so imperfect and flightsome
   with ritual
  as imperfection might have us want:

the body knows
    what shabby thorns we all manage—it knows
what is given, passed and outresonant: it knows

as it stretches, braves into a deep, wriggles into
   a horrible perception,

       ROOTING IS A DISTANT VISIT, something well-nigh
put off

When you see him
his face no more
determined than thousands
it sours
your own face—perhaps an awareness
it is a victory

to be subject there, throwing or leeching
　　realizing (as darkness first
　　　　　　moults
　　　　　　　　beneath his
　　　　　　cadillac; then
　　　　　　becomes an elegy for a woman, unknown,
　　　　who never turned an eye
　　　　　　　　or rifled a lover's
　　dream:

It is hard to be up there, hard
to be bluff-high
seeing yourself, thrown inward,
always in miniature: in the discovery when tallow leaks, eye
　　brings it filmy, the prodigy
seems but a freak
　　wondering among all the animations: and yet loving
all those awkward, weak-tongued scavengers, loving them
　　for the balls it took
to long there, jelly-eyed, in front of all
　　hysteria: indeed

all that makes one doubt. Loving them
　　as Liston loved you (you see this now) see the gleam, the
passage, the hustle
　　　　　　　　to wisdom: But now I think

as you are waiting for judgment
as you are just
about to pass into the nameless: just now
you understand the territory. You wish

like any father to explain it. You wish
there were words, small punches, anything
which might tell
them it is stony, sweat-hard, onerous
that
procuring is only half
the bargain:

Now
with the belt, with the dream flat
against your gut, you must begin
(like the creation you are)
to guild country, circumstance
by which the next may be brought forward.

Sanctifications

for Gwen Brooks

To love yourself
is an act unconditional:
a surrendering to no higher form or forum
than your evolution, sustenance:

So when
that pale, sickly thing
(the world a dead drum in his eyes)
demands of you a new slavery:

Remember, remember:
to love yourself
is an act unconditional: the first
learning in the wind

A Few Things Explained
(a small fable)

The rent was paid on the house
    or so the father
carefully explained—and the mother

lounging about in her bright, talcum-lipped
    buxom
dishabille
      told it
    to the children:

and the youngest (barely five years
          from the opening)
      juice welling
       from his nose
     barely gave it a thought:

and one day
    a man came
and he looked at the father
    and he succored the wife's
full underplanning
    and turned
away at the violence
    of the child's nasty nose

and this man
      came for
his house — had a piece

of paper, said
    it was his
       that the land, the foundation

everything that held
       or beset
brick or stepping stone: all
          was his

And the family had a few things explained
     and the father
        cried in the low
     magnolia
           and the mother resoundingly grabbed up her clothing
             and the little boy (as it was advisable for him
                to do) went meekly to the new
man, the landowner, and called him
          father.

From a Silent Center

From such country as I have seen
I would not
dare
speech
but rather
like a ferny breakout or an escaped
preface
disseminate
among city
folk, practice

deprivations of hemisphere
    where they seem to be
nothing:
        where they seem to return
            from the floodless ground—
    where they (out of breath and thin-celled)
        cull the disproportionate
            darkness—the hungered, the raving, the blown
    heavenward: the people in whom
                    I speak
                and love

and still, at dusk, the children
    feather the streets, see the options wearied
            in their gaunt, prideful
        mothers—in their strut, their ineffable
        continuing, in their ever-working, low-paid, boundless
    industry: but the pride

                like rum, like most city things quickly summoned
            and as quickly compost
                is made
            barren at the wheel of will:

I don't want to
    reduce
 them
            I don't want to call
        them low

No. It is just when time
        seems to loiter
    for an eternity
        when the trim banners
    of a furthering
  seem duffed: when no Jihad
opens the conceived
        to distention, the reedy creek
  to overswells
    of mudwallow:

I can understand a woman
I can understand
when her body
coils with the traipse of varience
coils
with the august
implication
of limit
and with the lone providence of any trapped thing
inches at the world of its fence

The Child

The clarity falls away:
I have given myself to the trees, to the spent
have let the damp and boggy places
wear thin
the mind put a small

bird in the dark. Nowhere
is he singing, nowhere
is there a dark center for him
for his vexed and ruling

voice. I've talked
of nothing: I've given him barely
an excuse, nothing of more
dazzle than what I've seen
and I have seen only

the low warble under the tree.
I've said
that the meek
urging under a leaf
is no more
than the sound of a lovesick

curious old man: no more
than fire eating at rust
no more
than a child

who cries and shakes us

And when the tree seems to fail
its stem
already branchless, its nubs belimbed
and lifeless, its sheer places
like some pure sexless thing
I understand what we want: a sexless
loving—no dirt, no pain, no weak

Knees. But I have seen that child
bending to the water
he has heard my feet; they seem like bombs
from the air, he has
looked me up and down
he has held me for a moment
to my life.

Saturday Night

Like something out of a Diane
Arbus photograph
they harrow
and
like the flamed bush, the forty
days healed in heaven and dialectic
they choke the lobed earth:

and there is always snow
we went to see Hamlet
the film
where speech was cut, the perfect
locution,
like a witless dog, wafted
hunger born, ending
in the indelicate
way one loans money to one's father:

Saturday night
seems ever to point
to a rarer side: we are not
of them; we are not—
as the snow falls, collects, refracts—snow people
we are not, though I find myself
still soughing
among the loose, sore rubble
of defections, mind cities, the layered (and oh so white, oh so
        beautiful) comminglings of sentience:

                and I speak
            of harried love, gallowed sex, the world
        so badly turned on itself
                that the only song
            is murder, death:

and yesterday, when I saw the children
        at the university I
    watched them swell into their fathers'
        faces
    like a poisoned ark

I am not
ever going
to make it:

I
am
different
I see
Black
they see Caribbean
I see
slave, me
and there is more
bone
to cut
I see
that there is more

And it is Saturday
it is snowing
Hamlet is looping away
it is snowing in
the fields, the calves of Joyce's drunken horse
it is snowing
and the warm feeling
of presence the warm
shall shake these people
to the stone

Today, Tomorrow

When you come out (and you are beautiful, earth-rich this
    morning)
it is necessary that I see you
jellied at the knees, your body
manganous like an old trawler
lumbering in its black
fishless bays:
or a great tanker, its insides
telling
like the plundered prophesy of widows:

And when I look at your face
which has barely a finger or welt of age
barely
a weed
out placed from a governance
I must turn my thought to the storm that gathers

Soon what is knowledge
shall have little
precision:
soon
muscles that so easily, greedily, walk
the sway-bridge over cricket
gab
and jam themselves
into the hem and body
will turn
flabby and sour, the chest

will move with misprehension, the key will not
   amble so petulant, stop signs
      will like fog-fouled rocks
dart
    dangerously out of the trees
as if they had found themselves: and yes

I hope that on that day
   as we rouse each other, meet the juggler of the daily, see
      the sawdust, upwellings and cornices
   so loosely cohered
     as to be almost
        not venerable

   (at the last we come round to the beginning)

And yet of a massing I hope
   our walk shall find the sea uplifting, the love of rocks
and shore-song too plentiful, the appreciation of that first
   shrill breeze whipping through our hands
     as never to leave us

Goodbye

Coming where sky
   is a dusty, strained bowl
birds furnish and thrill
          in hard, whirling nature

and there is no little thing
   not of taking, no animal
above the blood, no flower, snake, mandible
     no short, grumpy firefly
that has not been shaved, gored, derattled
     de-evidenced
or met with no closer
        appreciation than meat
    is meat
and living is meat by meat
   and in all there is the singing and the sung:

and nothing
   can urge me past
such sorrow as I think
   of your dead eyes, your country:

Oh, there is nothing born or living: longing

38

to make out in that
    airy utterance
that dancing of bowels:
    where do I stand
        where do
I

that deep foundering of your throat
    no resolve, no flitter of the adam's apple
      that loveless moment
        when you rose and spoke
      and nothing—no love, no devotion
          no simple pure sorting of what matters
      could shake you.

TO HEAR THE RIVER

Winter

Now the earth seems profound and inangular:
the shapes rise muted and interdependent: a tree's
limbs drool on the frame of a Volkswagen: a nest
swims frozen, well placed in a river's midst.
All the world is new shrapnel.

Winter seems to bind us in our ways:
suspended in whatever state of elegance or denial,
we are what we are: an acceptance.
And the most beautiful is just that:
a face which at last might be seen.

It is a time of chorus, of witness:
the few living things, bedraggled, light-sparse
wander in a world held back, inexpressible:
the few living things (memory-kept)
seem to falter, inbreak, though they shall not go under.

The Judge
for Bruce Wright

The judge, as he is good, wants to listen, accept.
He sees in the eyes of this straggler
much: a premature darkening, a closing
of the room to wonder: all the evidence
of sorrow—the way breakfast came, was washed down:

The judge remembers
how doubt often seemed a saving, a birdcage
raised in poolhalls and supple
thighs: how the street
seemed to drone in the head.
The blues, the hot lonesomes, the lame
nights when nothing would promise.

The judge turns into this young face
and sees the heat
of capitalism; he knows his voice
is worthy
if only it might surge
through knives:

Now his reason
ambles, grows stony, deepens:
The judge (accountable only to life)
sees this boy, a bent sapling, a rich stem
which need not break.

Family

It is with family
where all this begins: vexing, troubled
a slight bridge
over which all passes, is carried:

There are always dangers
when one speaks of large things; they are
irrefutable, the soul's barter, the last
improvisation before the downward rushing: and I know
fitted well for loss, fitted well
for ministry, fitted well for placing
the least image
where it will not befall
kingdoms—and I have fun
    with prophecy: I see the flame twitter, grow small,
                calm: I watch the narrow
        waters turn the headlong, near-arid beach
            into water's country: and I am not defiant, moony:

        And I am not the least in this: I am
            that I shall stand here
            waiting for the ceaseless tongues
                to somehow speak it, to make it known:

When one tries
to cover one's tracks
they hone a swath, larger, more evangelical
than a star's axis: Come and look

I know everything protects it own waffling.
So it is with poets. To keep darkness
intact I invite the substance (loas)

by which all that governs me is kept
intact: I inveigle everything: wood, flat-worm, child's play.

As interstellar, there is no family
but what is aloof with radiance—one sees only
what shines, beckons. And as I see it (all too morn-tossed)
had I not crossed into the thick weeds, had I
not seen the hour as one of tending
I might not have offered this:

There is nothing but creation: nothing
but shapes, waxings, wizenings, chrysalises.
And should one wonder whom to blame—the state, world,
    the ominous
weight of balance—all are guilty; all *need*

But this is a shaky flower, an abdication.
As we walk, hand in hand, the night mirrors more
than a healthy sunset, a gay abacus.
Rochelle and I
(now besides ourselves, a spreading of branches) understand:

Though much seems to be broken
as we pass
nothing is diminutive, tottering: with love
whatever imaginings we yield to
(be they in warm spring or seen at the mouth of cities)
climb with the gravest surety of angels.

Owls

Now the owls are flying
over the kept and dismal
houses, the college:

The owls are flying
out of the graveyards, out of the images
which provide for childhood; out
of the widening reasonableness, the thickets of wisdom:

The town is dark, the owls
fly over West Hill, the steeple, the last
mitigation before my house—the owls are flying
past the river, downward into the orchard:

The owls are flying, a winter
here always,a grey bulb
which will not grow addled or plow under.

Sacred Head

Yesterday I went looking for a room
I went
up and down stairs
in and out of elaborate
masonry, through and behind
girders, and it was always:
"We have no room."

And to an intelligent man (I like to think
of myself as such), finding
no place to put one's head
should be a particular problem, something
with a literary heralding:

But yesterday, just like the millions
of times they shunned me, moved too slowly
to cut the high-priced pizza, called me "nigger"
in word or action, I again knew something.

And someone who too easily rests
his head on white feathers (his belief that an antidote exists)
may find his ease uprooted, this
smart, quiet-looking black man finally having enough of it,
nigger, nigger, nigger, the world again swilling with blood.

Worms

The underworld must have its say:
the worms driven up
turn a dead lying to the season: they hang
outstretched, exiled:

Fleeing and lost, moving
inward and outward, the earth
(so often a friend) has turned them
out:

Now a full leaf
rises like prophecy   Somehow
they climb on: instinctual,
even as the world squirms
half-mad, dispersive:

In a sense beyond imagination
leaf becomes globe: and holding on
how easily a body manages!

Thinking of Octavio Paz

What grows weak and thin is the world tonight
as the long hiatus between scene and sense, bird and headlong
betrayal, as speech seems to hurl out
guiding nothing, forcing nothing back:

The waves of separation alive in the trees
(abstraction, dangerous when we tell of loss)
but it is the confluence, the freakery of vision, the violence
which is the truth of pain. Certainly reality

Exists, the stars fidgety like a life:
But how quickly I am full of myself, how easily
air fills and withdraws: this is the time of the uneasy truce,
the body hungering, fingering only its truth, disgust.

To Hear the River

for Langston Hughes

To hear
to hear
to hear the
to hear the strong
black song
to hear it—to hear the river
is to know

its ways: to know
the gaunt-thin
source which somehow
like Hughes
becomes long black water, becomes
(so that much might come after it)
a handhold, a griot:

And so long black song
comes dark, provident, absolute:

And finally coming to the river, facing
the dogs and white men, facing what is lost
and possible, *we hear the river, we hear
the river, we hear the river*

Snow

What peregrinations the mind
builds in shallow clusters, constellations:
the dropping of a lower
orb, a lesser deity, the first frost

inches on the willow: the spruce
cut back is not
cut out, and the thickening, gored
arch in the maple, thickening.

At the Bridge with Rufus
for James Baldwin

Once again the wind is howling and you, Rufus,
shall take that long shoreless journey back,
back into life, back where the alleys seem silent glaciers, the
    trees
bare indexes of themselves: Rufus, once again the wind howls
      and you remove yourself beyond any music:

Rufus, you hear the river: it calls
like some ill-fashioned gravity, a pact
honed when the stomach gnarled for bread—when you
(your own voice an accompaniment) forgot
      your family, forgot us, *forgot*
that we wrapped you in wind-tough sacrament, kept you
      (as we would others of prophecy):

But Rufus, you left us like a syphilitic:
you forgot the *beat*, the rich thump, the arpeggio
      which makes the knees jelly: Rufus,
         when the river called, you should have looked thither,
         let
the walls quake, the loneliness
      swim out some side window: But I understand

The river is strong at its source. Dangerous
it moves us past what we know.
I, too, have crept to that high place and looked outward.
Yes, it is hell. Yes, the voices open
like sweet music: and you, always you, the wind, the scream
$$\text{for blood:}$$

And you, Rufus, the last symbol.

Rufus, heroes *live*.
And you, fulfilling that other exactitude (showing how the
    axis pulls
equally, plunges into worlds and afterworlds): Rufus, you
    showed us
not how to live but how mighty the cost:

Rufus, you gave yourself to the wind.
It howls.
You gave yourself.
And the rest of us must go back to the dark city.

Morning

When you awake, when you ask the world
bristling with sunlight, what is
yours: you ask

What millions before (skittish before disaster)
have also asked: you link yourself
with time, ethos, passage. You might
prefer it otherwise. You think

Revelation shames like a ghost.
Yet when something leaves, it is not turned out of life.
Pieces do not so easily disassociate.
A stone falls throughout the universe.

This is real; it is not mystical.
Though I would like to make it understandable,
to lay it at your feet like a sheaf of roses,
there is something equally pulling:

For as the sun loosens in the mind
it shines somewhere far more intimately: it breaks
in that much-hidden and yet irrepressible world
where music is a body speaking

The Sea Brings Up Voices

for Genevieve

Now is the time for waking and making do: the sea
is the only surety, lover:
the sea, singing always, singing beyond:

It is an hour when one thinks of swimming or under-
mining, of surfaces and interiors: of paintings
where art places no boundary on dreams or love:

And though I whittle away at the frontier
the sea always brings up voices

Song: A Chant

for Michael Harper

What is most difficult
is to believe:

I say what is most difficult
is to believe:

When the sun
rises in the low, hard
grass

What is most difficult
is to believe:

When moon
comes night-certain
to the lake

What is most difficult
is to believe:

That Black children
gather a dream in their arms
and set that dream like a voice in their heads:
a vision so perfect, so inviolable
a man might wade
through centuries with an undeniable reverence, a love:

What is most difficult
is to believe:

And son and daughter
once were son and daughter
are son and daughter

What is most difficult
is to believe:

And Black people
shall see sun
forever, the world inexhaustible,
the possibilities
infinite like a Joshua tree or jazz:

What is most difficult
is to believe, I say:

What is most difficult
is to believe:

And believe we did
as the world urged us onward
to shine, shout, our music the only truth
in this dead, forgotten city.

Sunday Morning

At the center it all doesn't
matter: I've said it before. I've
tried all those things which promise to save
us, I mean, I've waded through the tennis

motionings, have roosted in
the pale ambiences (glass always warm
in hand), have
crisscrossed my family, darkened every
hatching of life, blotched even the sour
last thought of a prisoner. Nothing:

Nothing has given anything back.
I was thinking it is sad
that we see the world in language: we don't
really know the wind, the thornberry, the raccoon

who so easily slips from country
to city: who grows fat in the sewers: who
realizes that a life is a life.

And I would walk along the Hudson,
see the condoms swelling
like ghosts, envision some aspect best not
included, reasoned with. I don't like

myself. I don't trust
a voice which so glibly
flashes in the morning, titillating in the absolute
denial of what is.

This is not pretty. It is a building
which stops short of its architect, a child
who finds his only need is air
and that breath fails.

Harlem

for Gwendolyn Brooks

The wind sings in the slow
trees, while kids swim
in and out of being
like shards of imagination:

The great river muscles, the mythic salmon
gather at insects: the world of living
and plunging out of life
moves in a ceaseless mechanism:

In Harlem they are flung wide
in the streets. One vision
a barren truce, a taut-string, a blue collage; the other,
more beautiful, giddy, a life among ashes.

The Blues Singer

for Eleanor Traylor

She circles, a faithful novitiate:
she believes
her body tightly
pulling against
its grave surety: her arms
about to engage
the fall, the rushing downward:

Blues are her world; they sweep
out of her mouth
like cotton, like sun
drowned in the earth:

The blues are her:
they hang in the tress, scar
like children who go down to the river
and never come back—like we
who go down into the avenues
and do not return:

She hears
a high dangerous moon, a sadness:

Someone shall wander
like a worm's silk skin
as the wind of lilac
sucks it to the river.

Police and the Near Doomed Society

for Abdul

In Washington they throw him up against a wall,
their police bodies stiff, their intelligence
burdensome, sexual. They need
a *nigger's* head. They need it like a woman,
like something to grunt into.

And you, Abdul, here for what seems an endless
winter must be their need. They eye you
as you leave, books in hand, your thin, well-raced limbs
moving too easily for someone
Black in America.
They grunt. They see skull. They need to bust
a nigger's head. It is something
they barely understand, something
almost instinctual, as a cat sends out claws at the intimation
of falling.

They would do this to their wives.
(If there is love anywhere in this place
it is seen here. It speaks in the flanks. It
has little to do with gender.)
They would make her
climb. They would
have the blood push
out into the stinging air.

Abdul, we cannot continue to hold them.
Culture is not this thin-celled funk, this spiritless doom, this
interminable scream for blood, Blackblood, yellowblood,
deadeyes.

Deaths in this city do not matter: the West
is a great leaching ground, a lake
where the dead voice recriminations, are not
dead: I've seen them in the strangest outposts.

Someday the white children will hear it. They will hear it
     and awake.
Finally, Abdul, they will hear it and awake.

Beebe Lake*

Always I round your shoals (such blue-black,
    unyielding waters)
mulling something, lifting the last
stench of an idea, a mullah
among the detritus—and always
you stand
stagnant, ready to belch
out something useful, something which only
long grazing with the dead
permits:

I have come here
singing of my own prison, a fence
which has brought me back, stumbling, air-weary, blighted
like my friends
who believe—their faces as black as mine—that some dead
white dance, some slim opening
is the way outward: and trying
to burn up the least
hold of it—trying to prune
out every middling infatuation, every aping, every
waterlogged lust for Bach, Camelot, Shostakovich, I
come again to your shores:

But there is something
sweetly singing in your waters, sweetly
drifting out of
oily grass: here, you have seen it all; here you have
watched them tether
the long grass to an icy
destruction: you have seen as the hands have touched, grown
splotchy, finally lifting in some awful ambivalence:

64

You tell me
sitting as you have for tens of man-
made years, your basin
etched for beauty, your true beauty
rooted in the long
ways you have seen them come
and muster:

Watching you
I know it is a beauty
that man offers: it is not Mozart
who is responsible for the vatic climbing; not Dante
for the stairway; not Dostoevski for the ringing
down below.
I've heard it all. These men
have set your shoals to singing. *Sing then, sing.*

★a man-made body of water abutting Cornell University.

65

Song: A Motion of History
for Cecil

Once more I've begun the treatise; once more
I shall place my thoughts at the foci of wisdom
moving in that inner wheel, hoping like Ezekiel
that the patterns of nature—the laws
shall let my orbit stand:

I'm speaking about time and continents.
I'm speaking about what it exacted, borne, and somehow
    carried. I'm speaking about
the world of our fathers: the song and the past song:

And much has been asked of song. Don't
doubt it. Like love, like jazz, like the endless
visions which give us a life, song
is an awesome thing.
We must not betray it.
There is grief; there is grief enough.

So I think of Tanner's boy, kneeling
at his grandfather's knee, kneeling at the wide
mouth of guitar, the strongest source:

Free, intimate with time, burdened and lightened,
finally carried in a sea, a motion, a music: nothing
may turn him around. Listen:
the music is ours; it will not abandon us.

These Halves Are Whole

New Poems

The Music of Hunger

How delicately the blossoms fall
Over the fence, the bruised stones, the lap-
World which keeps out, who knows what.

How delicately the blossoms fall:
And I think of Harlem, that tree-balked country,
Where my brother dresses,
Hungry for the end of the world:

He is not on dope, scag; he is not
(however the facts may translate) fodder
For some furiously driven despot, a selfless husk
spinning with each new further exile:

Here one sees the soul's burden
Its great helplessness as it rages
Like a child
At the raw, rasped edge of self:

Here
in the ghetto
one sees the full eyes of foodlessness.

Dreams of Wholeness

Hearing the winter warbler's
twisting song
(the highest plaint of a life in halves)

We are reminded
of that other lover
(somewhere walking the world)

And our limbs take whole
steps to follow her
forgetting that we trekked

This way once, forgetting
that the winter warbler
sings always

1619–1979 Is A Large Time

1

When we came here, we knew it would not be easy.
Our language looked for a star, a galaxy,
Something to give us a dim penetration.
When we understood, many of us lost ourselves.

2

This morning was a blue morning:
Not a thing seemed rich or outlandish; my spirit
Dry as a man inched-up with heroin.
This morning I thought I might never leave here.

3

I count the blues; I count each and every one of them.
Children ask me what I recall, remember.
I remember their mother's bellies. I remember how small
Grew those ships which brought us here.

4

I count the blues; I count each and every one of them

5

Here, our children meet death
as one might the sun:
When we understood, many
of us lost ourselves.

6

Children ask me what I recall, remember

I leave from a boat, move to a great land
and wander to a newer forest.

7

The blues shall set you free
The blues shall set you free
The blues shall set you free
But I've been here so long

Gristle and Celebration

for Mari Evans

Soon there will be a fire out by the wind's hedge
and the small outhouse, thatched with promises, will run
over with the taint of slack water, turd:
Soon the land will clear again and disavow all building,
believing, like our ancestors, that one forever creates,
    that the sluice
is an uncorkable sieve—the world, all gristle and celebration:

Soon the hummingbird will perform his miracle,
outdoing the business of flying, his wings
rightfully fearful of pause, an endless barter
with a ceaseless problem: *how to stay afloat:* and I
shall spread my wicker thoughts out near the shallow creek,

forgetting that I am not of this place, that the sweet
swill of daisy or the second accurate love-thrust of woodcock
(each loving a minute a day later, as if the expectation
    somehow minutely
darkened): forgetting this and a thousand other rhapsodies
    of instinct,
I realize that this city self, so long a creature of window
    prophesy,
can sustain and broaden, withstand and withhold.

A World of Hedges

At the window the moth
flutters to be let inside

and I inside
flutter to meet him

and it seems the window
like an arid membrane

is at the center
of violation:

two violences: one wanting
to free self momentarily; the other

a self, ravishing self,
wishing only to fly further, farther

Harlem

So I awakened in the world, with a new danger.
Sight does that: it affords much,
but it destroys what little we had
surmised:

So I walked by a narrow stream
and kicked ice into a focus, and wondered
if anything felt my imposition: if anything
knew how tenaciously I tried to claim it.

When I look at how people survive:
how one can addle in a villa, another
dream in a shit-hole walk-up, I understand
more than words allow.

Though I know that the world changes little,
I find myself always knowing less than that.
Were chaos a trickle of water, I would come
proposing a river: yes, such is the way I maintain:

But when I saw him in the city,
when I watched him open the window
and let the sun in, secretly, with a minor yelp,
the sun shone—shone even on a dead, weedless river.

Daybreak

Clearly justice is the slow availing of winter:
how derationalized beyond any meaning, it oozes
into everything, seeming to be inoffensive, seeming
to have no odor, ritual: but the world misses

no chance to begin that awesome conjuring:
and narrowly collected (like a fire raised in sand)
nothing can come of it—nothing but what was
    inextinguishable,
intercellular: when the voice first roared

I was mindful that I had no understanding, that it came
like something hastily perceived but nonetheless
    extraordinary,
like something rehearsed for a pilgrimage without grammar.
Yet still I saw the bluejay

squawk at the appearance of ice, his ribs rounding
to take it all in, realizing that if his ribs can carry it,
it can be borne: and then a sudden surge of wind
carried his sound into the leaves: and still the squawk

fighting at the edge of it, loosening to the greater bulk
of announcement, for the first time admitting
that it might be uncontainable, unassimilable: and then
    the squawk,
like the most delicate trill in the universe

Yore
for Robert Hayden

When we ring round the campfire
it's time
to lodge the soft
nourishing belly
of history
to tell
and re-
tell
to harvest and resurplant:

for the voices (gone out and awash)
    bloat dull:
        the crop-warm hands
    remote like a chilling flood, a ballistic rock
                come not
in the least long viewing: come not
            where the swill
      is a rich
    crying, a tree
           winnowing, bearing up:

and as we grope
        noon-telling around the fire
blood hies in our veins
            and the one
                (darker and less morn-tossed) able
        to keep it in, to dominate it
            seems to slumber:

but the cargo
        aloose in his dreams
    swelters like a galley
        barreling into
Jamestown: too much quivering in its hold
                to keep.

Mother

Mother, it is always in this walk
        down the stairs
when I first see you
        and the small, half-steps
which have been your way, your life

and the madman you saw
        painting a clever rose for you (he hadn't painted a thing
            in five years: he was so full
                    of so much divinity
            that color seemed to retreat from him
like a road bludgeoned through embers)

Look behind that tree
        They are trying to get me
One of them He
            has a knife
They are between the tires
        We've got to go uptown: No, not by the bus
They are there also

And then you were in the street
        dad flew out of his office
I called him
    he knew at once:

The policemen were keeping
    the throng back
it seemed as if all the city were here:
A Puerto Rican lady
    said she had seen you before
        you were always nice, decent
    another continued:

She's crazy   She just fell out in the street   Says
crazy things about poison

The police were listening
        jotting down in their notebooks
TIME: PLACE: HEIGHT: COMPLEXION: *Black*

        Doctor, we didn't know what to do

Later, we came to see you
    you moved slowly like an elephant, your eyes swivelling
        like the lights of a passing truck

I don't want you here
I don't want you here
Get the nurse out   She plugs me with gas
I've seen the way she leers at me from the booth
and the doctor—you, my family—you've put me with this Italian
    he saw me on T.V.   He knows the guy
        who painted me a flower. He spoke to him.

Mother, I see the painting you did
    a snake drying on a stone
your mind has done some wonderful things:

    I remember those long hours
swinging in buses—how people
        knew me by your hand
                you
                you were good
                too good

            Don't be so good
            they will kill you

79

Don't be so good
they will kill you

Mother, this world
   is a sad, crazed place
      the best are thrown into holes, the others
silent madmen
   who know nothing
but that the skiff comes, waits, and brings them forever to
                                    Eden:

Yesterday, I went to look at your paintings
there was one, a large one
(it was Menemsha)
and the fishing boats were clearing
the harbor
and all above were birds:

And I remember you walking the beach
your straw hat tight
on your head, your curls
(the pride of Black Boston)
inviting even the dreamless to stir:

Yesterday you walked slowly down the steps
     kissed dad, Paul, Adrienne and me
and went to the coffee
       (the world a gay jaunt, Ellington in your
             strut, Ellington everywhere):

And yesterday I saw something shining
     in your eyes
        and it may not last long.

Now the Stones Sing

Now the windrow of stones
sings its leaves barren:

And I wonder about the ceaseless
offerings, about the soul

which sheds light
like a million planets:

All this I wonder about
as the wind-thick maple showers

its leaves downward
much like a waterless divining

hones to the spirit's
invisible seas.

The Black Intellectual

for W.E.B. DuBois

We have shored up so much
to keep from rioting.   To keep it down
we move in and out of our skins
in some grotesque obeisance, some wretching of our forms
as if we were addled neon signs.

Indeed we are afraid of ourselves.
Riding in the least seat, in the last car, in the longest
train is still riding; it is safe.
Powers still mightily discipline the universe: and gods
(be they august or sweet) provide a cadence.

Yet when I walk near their big clovered houses,
see their doom-eyed children, watch
their ornamental boats flounder in the river, I
want to save them.

And when they press
me in class, when they want
to know how soil is gathered, how earth
shares so little, I find myself answering:

But sometimes the other voice in me
heaves from the gut.
Cold, defiant, persuasive
it seems to hold everything: Attica
Soweto, Chile, Little Rock, Mozambique:

And now I see nothing in their stunted lives
but death; I see nothing in their hopeless
celebration but blood; I see nothing but the ceaseless waste
of dark bodies, piling up as they ask:

the questions always coming, always coming
as if questions might stop it. Today I have given up
answering: today I no longer look upon or care about the easy
offerings to insatiable gods: today
should a wind swell on the river and wrack their foundering
                                                         boat
I might only wish that all were present.

Winter Song
for Rochelle

It is the barest turn of season
when the mind, drawn into
the darkest landscape

is a forgotten tower, a song
waffling over the ribs
like a drowned boat:

Still it is winter's song
when ice shares
its sovereign, soulless light.

An Edge of Thanks

The snow is not yet a reality here:
and the first yawing of daisy, slightly overcome,
cannot be taken as a reckoning:

And though the wild-rose is gone,
the long-held rare song of a warbler
rises like a stairway:

Always, absently though irrepressibly,
this wintry world
wanders from the knife to the cross.

Meditation at Jones River

When the river swells, the loose
soarings of loon betray
how difficult the singing: but if one looks
beyond the mist, how the willows keep

it fast and upwind: how they bend
disk-shaped, resonative, frantic that the song be heard:
and even the inlet, a natural tuning fork,
will not let the slightest voice suffer silent.